THE LORD'S DEVOTIONAL JOURNAL

FOR THE COMMITTED CHRISTIAN

Activinotes

Activinotes

DAILY JOURNALS, PLANNERS, NOTEBOOKS AND OTHER BLANK BOOKS

This Book Belongs To

_____

Devotional

Today is_____

I'm feeling	I'm thinking about

Realizations

MY TIME WITH THE LORD

date: _____

scriptures: _____ devotionals: _____

What the Lord said to me today:

_____
_____
_____
_____
_____
_____
_____
_____
_____
_____
_____

Dear Lord,

_____
_____
_____
_____
_____
_____
_____
_____
_____
_____
_____
_____

Prayer Requests:

_____
_____
_____

Action Items:

_____
_____
_____
_____

MY TIME WITH THE LORD

date: _____

scriptures: _____ devotionals: _____

What the Lord said to me today:

_____
_____
_____
_____
_____
_____
_____
_____
_____
_____
_____

Dear Lord,

_____
_____
_____
_____
_____
_____
_____
_____
_____
_____
_____
_____
_____

Prayer Requests:

_____
_____
_____

Action Items:

_____
_____
_____
_____

MY TIME WITH THE LORD

date: _____

scriptures: _____ devotionals: _____

What the Lord said to me today:

_____
_____
_____
_____
_____
_____
_____
_____
_____
_____
_____

Dear Lord,

_____
_____
_____
_____
_____
_____
_____
_____
_____
_____
_____

Prayer Requests:

_____
_____
_____

Action Items:

_____
_____
_____
_____

MY TIME WITH THE LORD

date: _____

scriptures: _____ devotionals: _____

What the Lord said to me today:

_____
_____
_____
_____
_____
_____
_____
_____
_____
_____
_____

Dear Lord,

_____
_____
_____
_____
_____
_____
_____
_____
_____
_____
_____
_____

Prayer Requests:

_____
_____
_____

Action Items:

_____
_____
_____
_____

MY TIME WITH THE LORD

date: _____

scriptures: _____ devotionals: _____

What the Lord said to me today:

_____
_____
_____
_____
_____
_____
_____
_____
_____
_____
_____

Dear Lord,

_____
_____
_____
_____
_____
_____
_____
_____
_____
_____
_____

Prayer Requests:

_____
_____
_____

Action Items:

_____
_____
_____
_____

MY TIME WITH THE LORD

date: _____

scriptures: _____ devotionals: _____

What the Lord said to me today:

_____
_____
_____
_____
_____
_____
_____
_____
_____
_____
_____
_____

Dear Lord,

_____
_____
_____
_____
_____
_____
_____
_____
_____
_____
_____
_____
_____

Prayer Requests:

_____
_____
_____

Action Items:

_____
_____
_____
_____

MY TIME WITH THE LORD

date: _____

scriptures: _____ devotionals: _____

What the Lord said to me today:

_____
_____
_____
_____
_____
_____
_____
_____
_____
_____

Dear Lord,

_____
_____
_____
_____
_____
_____
_____
_____
_____
_____
_____
_____

Prayer Requests:

_____
_____
_____

Action Items:

_____
_____
_____
_____

MY TIME WITH THE LORD

date: _____

scriptures: _____ devotionals: _____

What the Lord said to me today:

_____
_____
_____
_____
_____
_____
_____
_____
_____
_____
_____

Dear Lord,

_____
_____
_____
_____
_____
_____
_____
_____
_____
_____
_____
_____

Prayer Requests:

_____
_____
_____

Action Items:

_____
_____
_____
_____

MY TIME WITH THE LORD

date: _____

scriptures: _____ devotionals: _____

What the Lord said to me today:

_____
_____
_____
_____
_____
_____
_____
_____
_____
_____
_____

Dear Lord,

_____
_____
_____
_____
_____
_____
_____
_____
_____
_____
_____
_____
_____

Prayer Requests:

_____
_____
_____

Action Items:

_____
_____
_____
_____

MY TIME WITH THE LORD

date: _____

scriptures: _____ devotionals: _____

What the Lord said to me today:

_____
_____
_____
_____
_____
_____
_____
_____
_____
_____
_____

Dear Lord,

_____
_____
_____
_____
_____
_____
_____
_____
_____
_____
_____

Prayer Requests:

_____
_____
_____

Action Items:

_____
_____
_____
_____

MY TIME WITH THE LORD

date: _____

scriptures: _____ devotionals: _____

What the Lord said to me today:

_____
_____
_____
_____
_____
_____
_____
_____
_____
_____
_____

Dear Lord,

_____
_____
_____
_____
_____
_____
_____
_____
_____
_____
_____

Prayer Requests:

_____
_____
_____

Action Items:

_____
_____
_____
_____

MY TIME WITH THE LORD

date: _____

scriptures: _____ devotionals: _____

What the Lord said to me today:

_____
_____
_____
_____
_____
_____
_____
_____
_____
_____

Dear Lord,

_____
_____
_____
_____
_____
_____
_____
_____
_____
_____
_____
_____

Prayer Requests:

_____
_____
_____

Action Items:

_____
_____
_____
_____

MY TIME WITH THE LORD

date: _____

scriptures: _____ devotionals: _____

What the Lord said to me today:

_____
_____
_____
_____
_____
_____
_____
_____
_____
_____

Dear Lord,

_____
_____
_____
_____
_____
_____
_____
_____
_____
_____
_____

Prayer Requests:

_____
_____
_____

Action Items:

_____
_____
_____
_____

MY TIME WITH THE LORD

date: _____

scriptures: _____ devotionals: _____

What the Lord said to me today:

_____
_____
_____
_____
_____
_____
_____
_____
_____
_____

Dear Lord,

_____
_____
_____
_____
_____
_____
_____
_____
_____
_____
_____

Prayer Requests:

_____
_____
_____

Action Items:

_____
_____
_____
_____

MY TIME WITH THE LORD

date: _____

scriptures: _____ devotionals: _____

What the Lord said to me today:

_____
_____
_____
_____
_____
_____
_____
_____
_____
_____
_____

Dear Lord,

_____
_____
_____
_____
_____
_____
_____
_____
_____
_____
_____
_____
_____

Prayer Requests:

_____
_____
_____

Action Items:

_____
_____
_____
_____

MY TIME WITH THE LORD

date: _____

scriptures: _____ devotionals: _____

What the Lord said to me today:

_____
_____
_____
_____
_____
_____
_____
_____
_____
_____
_____

Dear Lord,

_____
_____
_____
_____
_____
_____
_____
_____
_____
_____
_____
_____

Prayer Requests:

_____
_____
_____

Action Items:

_____
_____
_____
_____

MY TIME WITH THE LORD

date: _____

scriptures: _____ *devotionals:* _____

What the Lord said to me today:

_____
_____
_____
_____
_____
_____
_____
_____
_____
_____
_____

Dear Lord,

_____
_____
_____
_____
_____
_____
_____
_____
_____
_____
_____

Prayer Requests:

_____
_____
_____

Action Items:

_____
_____
_____
_____

MY TIME WITH THE LORD

date: _____

scriptures: _____ devotionals: _____

What the Lord said to me today:

_____
_____
_____
_____
_____
_____
_____
_____
_____
_____
_____

Dear Lord,

_____
_____
_____
_____
_____
_____
_____
_____
_____
_____
_____
_____
_____

Prayer Requests:

_____
_____
_____

Action Items:

_____
_____
_____
_____

MY TIME WITH THE LORD

date: _____

scriptures: _____ devotionals: _____

What the Lord said to me today:

_____
_____
_____
_____
_____
_____
_____
_____
_____
_____
_____

Dear Lord,

_____
_____
_____
_____
_____
_____
_____
_____
_____
_____
_____

Prayer Requests:

_____
_____
_____

Action Items:

_____
_____
_____
_____

MY TIME WITH THE LORD

date: _____

scriptures: _____ devotionals: _____

What the Lord said to me today:

_____
_____
_____
_____
_____
_____
_____
_____
_____
_____
_____

Dear Lord,

_____
_____
_____
_____
_____
_____
_____
_____
_____
_____
_____
_____

Prayer Requests:

_____
_____
_____

Action Items:

_____
_____
_____
_____

MY TIME WITH THE LORD

date: _____

scriptures: _____ devotionals: _____

What the Lord said to me today:

_____
_____
_____
_____
_____
_____
_____
_____
_____
_____
_____

Dear Lord,

_____
_____
_____
_____
_____
_____
_____
_____
_____
_____
_____
_____

Prayer Requests:

_____
_____
_____

Action Items:

_____
_____
_____
_____

MY TIME WITH THE LORD

date: _____

scriptures: _____ devotionals: _____

What the Lord said to me today:

_____
_____
_____
_____
_____
_____
_____
_____
_____
_____
_____

Dear Lord,

_____
_____
_____
_____
_____
_____
_____
_____
_____
_____
_____
_____

Prayer Requests:

_____
_____
_____

Action Items:

_____
_____
_____
_____

MY TIME WITH THE LORD

date: _____

scriptures: _____ *devotionals:* _____

What the Lord said to me today:

_____
_____
_____
_____
_____
_____
_____
_____
_____
_____

Dear Lord,

_____
_____
_____
_____
_____
_____
_____
_____
_____
_____
_____
_____

Prayer Requests:

_____
_____
_____

Action Items:

_____
_____
_____
_____

Devotional

Self-Improvement _____

Short-term goals	Long-term goals

Devotional

Today is _____

I'm feeling	I'm thinking about

Realizations

MY TIME WITH THE LORD

date: _____

scriptures: _____ devotionals: _____

What the Lord said to me today:

_____
_____
_____
_____
_____
_____
_____
_____
_____
_____
_____

Dear Lord,

_____
_____
_____
_____
_____
_____
_____
_____
_____
_____
_____
_____

Prayer Requests:

_____
_____
_____

Action Items:

_____
_____
_____
_____

MY TIME WITH THE LORD

date: _____

scriptures: _____ devotionals: _____

What the Lord said to me today:

_____
_____
_____
_____
_____
_____
_____
_____
_____
_____

Dear Lord,

_____
_____
_____
_____
_____
_____
_____
_____
_____
_____
_____

Prayer Requests:

_____
_____
_____

Action Items:

_____
_____
_____
_____

MY TIME WITH THE LORD

date: _____

scriptures: _____ devotionals: _____

What the Lord said to me today:

_____
_____
_____
_____
_____
_____
_____
_____
_____
_____
_____

Dear Lord,

_____
_____
_____
_____
_____
_____
_____
_____
_____
_____
_____
_____

Prayer Requests:

_____
_____
_____

Action Items:

_____
_____
_____
_____

MY TIME WITH THE LORD

date: _____

scriptures: _____ devotionals: _____

What the Lord said to me today:

_____
_____
_____
_____
_____
_____
_____
_____
_____
_____
_____

Dear Lord,

_____
_____
_____
_____
_____
_____
_____
_____
_____
_____
_____
_____

Prayer Requests:

_____
_____
_____

Action Items:

_____
_____
_____
_____

MY TIME WITH THE LORD

date: _____

scriptures: _____ devotionals: _____

What the Lord said to me today:

_____
_____
_____
_____
_____
_____
_____
_____
_____
_____
_____

Dear Lord,

_____
_____
_____
_____
_____
_____
_____
_____
_____
_____
_____
_____

Prayer Requests:

_____
_____
_____

Action Items:

_____
_____
_____
_____

MY TIME WITH THE LORD

date: _____

scriptures: _____ devotionals: _____

What the Lord said to me today:

_____
_____
_____
_____
_____
_____
_____
_____
_____
_____
_____

Dear Lord,

_____
_____
_____
_____
_____
_____
_____
_____
_____
_____
_____

Prayer Requests:

_____
_____
_____

Action Items:

_____
_____
_____
_____

MY TIME WITH THE LORD

date: _____

scriptures: _____ devotionals: _____

What the Lord said to me today:

_____
_____
_____
_____
_____
_____
_____
_____
_____
_____
_____

Dear Lord,

_____
_____
_____
_____
_____
_____
_____
_____
_____
_____
_____
_____

Prayer Requests:

_____
_____
_____

Action Items:

_____
_____
_____
_____

MY TIME WITH THE LORD

date: _____

scriptures: _____ devotionals: _____

What the Lord said to me today:

_____
_____
_____
_____
_____
_____
_____
_____
_____
_____

Dear Lord,

_____
_____
_____
_____
_____
_____
_____
_____
_____
_____
_____

Prayer Requests:

_____
_____
_____

Action Items:

_____
_____
_____
_____

MY TIME WITH THE LORD

date: _____

scriptures: _____ devotionals: _____

What the Lord said to me today:

_____
_____
_____
_____
_____
_____
_____
_____
_____
_____
_____

Dear Lord,

_____
_____
_____
_____
_____
_____
_____
_____
_____
_____
_____
_____

Prayer Requests:

_____
_____
_____

Action Items:

_____
_____
_____
_____

MY TIME WITH THE LORD

date: _____

scriptures: _____ devotionals: _____

What the Lord said to me today:

_____
_____
_____
_____
_____
_____
_____
_____
_____
_____

Dear Lord,

_____
_____
_____
_____
_____
_____
_____
_____
_____
_____
_____

Prayer Requests:

_____
_____
_____

Action Items:

_____
_____
_____

MY TIME WITH THE LORD

date: _____

scriptures: _____ *devotionals:* _____

What the Lord said to me today:

_____
_____
_____
_____
_____
_____
_____
_____
_____
_____

Dear Lord,

_____
_____
_____
_____
_____
_____
_____
_____
_____
_____

Prayer Requests:

_____
_____
_____

Action Items:

_____
_____
_____
_____

MY TIME WITH THE LORD

date: _____

scriptures: _____ devotionals: _____

What the Lord said to me today:

_____
_____
_____
_____
_____
_____
_____
_____
_____
_____
_____

Dear Lord,

_____
_____
_____
_____
_____
_____
_____
_____
_____
_____
_____
_____
_____

Prayer Requests:

_____
_____
_____
_____

Action Items:

_____
_____
_____
_____

MY TIME WITH THE LORD

date: _____

scriptures: _____ devotionals: _____

What the Lord said to me today:

_____
_____
_____
_____
_____
_____
_____
_____
_____
_____
_____

Dear Lord,

_____
_____
_____
_____
_____
_____
_____
_____
_____
_____
_____
_____

Prayer Requests:

_____
_____
_____

Action Items:

_____
_____
_____
_____

MY TIME WITH THE LORD

date: _____

scriptures: _____ devotionals: _____

What the Lord said to me today:

_____
_____
_____
_____
_____
_____
_____
_____
_____
_____
_____

Dear Lord,

_____
_____
_____
_____
_____
_____
_____
_____
_____
_____
_____

Prayer Requests:

_____
_____
_____

Action Items:

_____
_____
_____
_____

MY TIME WITH THE LORD

date: _____

scriptures: _____ devotionals: _____

What the Lord said to me today:

_____
_____
_____
_____
_____
_____
_____
_____
_____
_____
_____

Dear Lord,

_____
_____
_____
_____
_____
_____
_____
_____
_____
_____
_____

Prayer Requests:

_____
_____
_____

Action Items:

_____
_____
_____
_____

MY TIME WITH THE LORD

date: _____

scriptures: _____ devotionals: _____

What the Lord said to me today:

_____
_____
_____
_____
_____
_____
_____
_____
_____
_____
_____

Dear Lord,

_____
_____
_____
_____
_____
_____
_____
_____
_____
_____
_____
_____
_____

Prayer Requests:

_____
_____
_____

Action Items:

_____
_____
_____
_____

MY TIME WITH THE LORD

date: _____

scriptures: _____ devotionals: _____

What the Lord said to me today:

_____
_____
_____
_____
_____
_____
_____
_____
_____
_____
_____

Dear Lord,

_____
_____
_____
_____
_____
_____
_____
_____
_____
_____
_____
_____

Prayer Requests:

_____
_____
_____

Action Items:

_____
_____
_____
_____

MY TIME WITH THE LORD

date: _____

scriptures: _____ devotionals: _____

What the Lord said to me today:

_____
_____
_____
_____
_____
_____
_____
_____
_____
_____

Dear Lord,

_____
_____
_____
_____
_____
_____
_____
_____
_____
_____
_____
_____

Prayer Requests:

_____
_____
_____

Action Items:

_____
_____
_____
_____

MY TIME WITH THE LORD

date: _____

scriptures: _____ *devotionals:* _____

What the Lord said to me today:

_____
_____
_____
_____
_____
_____
_____
_____
_____
_____
_____

Dear Lord,

_____
_____
_____
_____
_____
_____
_____
_____
_____
_____
_____
_____

Prayer Requests:

_____
_____
_____

Action Items:

_____
_____
_____
_____

MY TIME WITH THE LORD

date: _____

scriptures: _____ devotionals: _____

What the Lord said to me today:

_____
_____
_____
_____
_____
_____
_____
_____
_____
_____

Dear Lord,

_____
_____
_____
_____
_____
_____
_____
_____
_____
_____
_____

Prayer Requests:

_____
_____
_____

Action Items:

_____
_____
_____
_____

MY TIME WITH THE LORD

date: _____

scriptures: _____ devotionals: _____

What the Lord said to me today:

_____
_____
_____
_____
_____
_____
_____
_____
_____
_____
_____

Dear Lord,

_____
_____
_____
_____
_____
_____
_____
_____
_____
_____
_____
_____

Prayer Requests:

_____
_____
_____

Action Items:

_____
_____
_____
_____

MY TIME WITH THE LORD

date: _____

scriptures: _____ devotionals: _____

What the Lord said to me today:

_____
_____
_____
_____
_____
_____
_____
_____
_____
_____
_____

Dear Lord,

_____
_____
_____
_____
_____
_____
_____
_____
_____
_____
_____
_____

Prayer Requests:

_____
_____
_____

Action Items:

_____
_____
_____
_____

MY TIME WITH THE LORD

date: _____

scriptures: _____ devotionals: _____

What the Lord said to me today:

_____
_____
_____
_____
_____
_____
_____
_____
_____
_____
_____

Dear Lord,

_____
_____
_____
_____
_____
_____
_____
_____
_____
_____
_____
_____

Prayer Requests:

_____
_____
_____

Action Items:

_____
_____
_____
_____

MY TIME WITH THE LORD

date: _____

scriptures: _____ devotionals: _____

What the Lord said to me today:

_____
_____
_____
_____
_____
_____
_____
_____
_____
_____
_____

Dear Lord,

_____
_____
_____
_____
_____
_____
_____
_____
_____
_____

Prayer Requests:

_____
_____
_____

Action Items:

_____
_____
_____
_____

MY TIME WITH THE LORD

date: _____

scriptures: _____ devotionals: _____

What the Lord said to me today:

_____
_____
_____
_____
_____
_____
_____
_____
_____
_____
_____

Dear Lord,

_____
_____
_____
_____
_____
_____
_____
_____
_____
_____
_____

Prayer Requests:

_____
_____
_____

Action Items:

_____
_____
_____
_____

MY TIME WITH THE LORD

date: _____

scriptures: _____ devotionals: _____

What the Lord said to me today:

_____
_____
_____
_____
_____
_____
_____
_____
_____
_____
_____

Dear Lord,

_____
_____
_____
_____
_____
_____
_____
_____
_____
_____
_____
_____

Prayer Requests:

_____
_____
_____

Action Items:

_____
_____
_____
_____

MY TIME WITH THE LORD

date: _____

scriptures: _____ devotionals: _____

What the Lord said to me today:

_____
_____
_____
_____
_____
_____
_____
_____
_____
_____
_____

Dear Lord,

_____
_____
_____
_____
_____
_____
_____
_____
_____
_____
_____
_____

Prayer Requests:

_____
_____
_____

Action Items:

_____
_____
_____
_____

MY TIME WITH THE LORD

date: _____

scriptures: _____ devotionals: _____

What the Lord said to me today:

_____
_____
_____
_____
_____
_____
_____
_____
_____
_____
_____

Dear Lord,

_____
_____
_____
_____
_____
_____
_____
_____
_____
_____
_____
_____

Prayer Requests:

_____
_____
_____

Action Items:

_____
_____
_____
_____

MY TIME WITH THE LORD

date: _____

scriptures: _____ devotionals: _____

What the Lord said to me today:

_____

_____

_____

_____

_____

_____

_____

_____

_____

_____

Dear Lord,

_____

_____

_____

_____

_____

_____

_____

_____

_____

_____

_____

Prayer Requests:

_____

_____

_____

Action Items:

_____

_____

_____

_____

MY TIME WITH THE LORD

date: _____

scriptures: _____ devotionals: _____

What the Lord said to me today:

_____
_____
_____
_____
_____
_____
_____
_____
_____
_____
_____

Dear Lord,

_____
_____
_____
_____
_____
_____
_____
_____
_____
_____
_____

Prayer Requests:

_____
_____
_____

Action Items:

_____
_____
_____
_____

MY TIME WITH THE LORD

date: _____

scriptures: _____ devotionals: _____

What the Lord said to me today:

_____
_____
_____
_____
_____
_____
_____
_____
_____
_____
_____

Dear Lord,

_____
_____
_____
_____
_____
_____
_____
_____
_____
_____
_____
_____

Prayer Requests:

_____
_____
_____

Action Items:

_____
_____
_____
_____

MY TIME WITH THE LORD

date: _____

scriptures: _____ devotionals: _____

What the Lord said to me today:

_____
_____
_____
_____
_____
_____
_____
_____
_____
_____

Dear Lord,

_____
_____
_____
_____
_____
_____
_____
_____
_____
_____
_____

Prayer Requests:

_____
_____
_____

Action Items:

_____
_____
_____

Devotional

Self-Improvement _____

Short-term goals	Long-term goals

Devotional

Today is_____

I'm feeling	I'm thinking about

Realizations

MY TIME WITH THE LORD

date: _____

scriptures: _____ devotionals: _____

What the Lord said to me today:

_____
_____
_____
_____
_____
_____
_____
_____
_____
_____
_____

Dear Lord,

_____
_____
_____
_____
_____
_____
_____
_____
_____
_____
_____
_____

Prayer Requests:

_____
_____
_____

Action Items:

_____
_____
_____
_____

MY TIME WITH THE LORD

date: _____

scriptures: _____ devotionals: _____

What the Lord said to me today:

_____
_____
_____
_____
_____
_____
_____
_____
_____
_____
_____

Dear Lord,

_____
_____
_____
_____
_____
_____
_____
_____
_____
_____
_____
_____

Prayer Requests:

_____
_____
_____

Action Items:

_____
_____
_____
_____

MY TIME WITH THE LORD

date: _____

scriptures: _____ devotionals: _____

What the Lord said to me today:

_____
_____
_____
_____
_____
_____
_____
_____
_____
_____
_____

Dear Lord,

_____
_____
_____
_____
_____
_____
_____
_____
_____
_____
_____
_____

Prayer Requests:

_____
_____
_____

Action Items:

_____
_____
_____
_____

MY TIME WITH THE LORD

date: _____

scriptures: _____ devotionals: _____

What the Lord said to me today:

_____
_____
_____
_____
_____
_____
_____
_____
_____
_____

Dear Lord,

_____
_____
_____
_____
_____
_____
_____
_____
_____
_____
_____

Prayer Requests:

_____
_____
_____

Action Items:

_____
_____
_____
_____

MY TIME WITH THE LORD

date: _____

scriptures: _____ devotionals: _____

What the Lord said to me today:

_____
_____
_____
_____
_____
_____
_____
_____
_____
_____

Dear Lord,

_____
_____
_____
_____
_____
_____
_____
_____
_____
_____
_____

Prayer Requests:

_____
_____
_____

Action Items:

_____
_____
_____
_____

MY TIME WITH THE LORD

date: _____

scriptures: _____ devotionals: _____

What the Lord said to me today:

_____
_____
_____
_____
_____
_____
_____
_____
_____
_____

Dear Lord,

_____
_____
_____
_____
_____
_____
_____
_____
_____
_____
_____

Prayer Requests:

_____
_____
_____

Action Items:

_____
_____
_____
_____

MY TIME WITH THE LORD

date: _____

scriptures: _____ devotionals: _____

What the Lord said to me today:

_____
_____
_____
_____
_____
_____
_____
_____
_____
_____
_____

Dear Lord,

_____
_____
_____
_____
_____
_____
_____
_____
_____
_____
_____
_____

Prayer Requests:

_____
_____
_____

Action Items:

_____
_____
_____
_____

MY TIME WITH THE LORD

date: _____

scriptures: _____ devotionals: _____

What the Lord said to me today:

_____
_____
_____
_____
_____
_____
_____
_____
_____
_____
_____

Dear Lord,

_____
_____
_____
_____
_____
_____
_____
_____
_____
_____
_____

Prayer Requests:

_____
_____
_____

Action Items:

_____
_____
_____
_____

MY TIME WITH THE LORD

date: _____

scriptures: _____ devotionals: _____

What the Lord said to me today:

_____
_____
_____
_____
_____
_____
_____
_____
_____
_____

Dear Lord,

_____
_____
_____
_____
_____
_____
_____
_____
_____
_____
_____

Prayer Requests:

_____
_____
_____

Action Items:

_____
_____
_____
_____

MY TIME WITH THE LORD

date: _____

scriptures: _____ devotionals: _____

What the Lord said to me today:

_____
_____
_____
_____
_____
_____
_____
_____
_____
_____
_____

Dear Lord,

_____
_____
_____
_____
_____
_____
_____
_____
_____
_____
_____
_____

Prayer Requests:

_____
_____
_____

Action Items:

_____
_____
_____
_____

MY TIME WITH THE LORD

date: _____

scriptures: _____ devotionals: _____

What the Lord said to me today:

_____
_____
_____
_____
_____
_____
_____
_____
_____
_____
_____

Dear Lord,

_____
_____
_____
_____
_____
_____
_____
_____
_____
_____
_____
_____

Prayer Requests:

_____
_____
_____

Action Items:

_____
_____
_____
_____

MY TIME WITH THE LORD

date: _____

scriptures: _____ *devotionals:* _____

What the Lord said to me today:

_____
_____
_____
_____
_____
_____
_____
_____
_____
_____
_____

Dear Lord,

_____
_____
_____
_____
_____
_____
_____
_____
_____
_____
_____
_____

Prayer Requests:

_____
_____
_____

Action Items:

_____
_____
_____
_____

MY TIME WITH THE LORD

date: _____

scriptures: _____ devotionals: _____

What the Lord said to me today:

_____
_____
_____
_____
_____
_____
_____
_____
_____
_____

Dear Lord,

_____
_____
_____
_____
_____
_____
_____
_____
_____
_____
_____
_____
_____

Prayer Requests:

_____
_____
_____

Action Items:

_____
_____
_____
_____

MY TIME WITH THE LORD

date: _____

scriptures: _____ devotionals: _____

What the Lord said to me today:

_____
_____
_____
_____
_____
_____
_____
_____
_____
_____
_____
_____

Dear Lord,

_____
_____
_____
_____
_____
_____
_____
_____
_____
_____
_____
_____

Prayer Requests:

_____
_____
_____

Action Items:

_____
_____
_____
_____

MY TIME WITH THE LORD

date: _____

scriptures: _____ devotionals: _____

What the Lord said to me today:

_____
_____
_____
_____
_____
_____
_____
_____
_____
_____
_____

Dear Lord,

_____
_____
_____
_____
_____
_____
_____
_____
_____
_____
_____
_____

Prayer Requests:

_____
_____
_____

Action Items:

_____
_____
_____
_____

MY TIME WITH THE LORD

date: _____

scriptures: _____ *devotionals:* _____

What the Lord said to me today:

_____
_____
_____
_____
_____
_____
_____
_____
_____
_____

Dear Lord,

_____
_____
_____
_____
_____
_____
_____
_____
_____
_____
_____

Prayer Requests:

_____
_____
_____

Action Items:

_____
_____
_____
_____

MY TIME WITH THE LORD

date: _____

scriptures: _____ *devotionals:* _____

What the Lord said to me today:

_____
_____
_____
_____
_____
_____
_____
_____
_____
_____

Dear Lord,

_____
_____
_____
_____
_____
_____
_____
_____
_____
_____
_____

Prayer Requests:

_____
_____
_____

Action Items:

_____
_____
_____
_____

MY TIME WITH THE LORD

date: _____

scriptures: _____ devotionals: _____

What the Lord said to me today:

_____
_____
_____
_____
_____
_____
_____
_____
_____
_____
_____

Dear Lord,

_____
_____
_____
_____
_____
_____
_____
_____
_____
_____
_____
_____
_____

Prayer Requests:

_____
_____
_____

Action Items:

_____
_____
_____
_____

MY TIME WITH THE LORD

date: _____

scriptures: _____ devotionals: _____

What the Lord said to me today:

_____
_____
_____
_____
_____
_____
_____
_____
_____
_____
_____

Dear Lord,

_____
_____
_____
_____
_____
_____
_____
_____
_____
_____
_____
_____
_____

Prayer Requests:

_____
_____
_____

Action Items:

_____
_____
_____
_____

MY TIME WITH THE LORD

date: _____

scriptures: _____ devotionals: _____

What the Lord said to me today:

_____
_____
_____
_____
_____
_____
_____
_____
_____
_____
_____

Dear Lord,

_____
_____
_____
_____
_____
_____
_____
_____
_____
_____
_____
_____

Prayer Requests:

_____
_____
_____

Action Items:

_____
_____
_____
_____

MY TIME WITH THE LORD

date: _____

scriptures: _____ devotionals: _____

What the Lord said to me today:

_____
_____
_____
_____
_____
_____
_____
_____
_____
_____
_____

Dear Lord,

_____
_____
_____
_____
_____
_____
_____
_____
_____
_____
_____
_____

Prayer Requests:

_____
_____
_____

Action Items:

_____
_____
_____
_____

MY TIME WITH THE LORD

date: _____

scriptures: _____ devotionals: _____

What the Lord said to me today:

_____
_____
_____
_____
_____
_____
_____
_____
_____
_____
_____

Dear Lord,

_____
_____
_____
_____
_____
_____
_____
_____
_____
_____
_____

Prayer Requests:

_____
_____
_____

Action Items:

_____
_____
_____
_____

MY TIME WITH THE LORD

date: _____

scriptures: _____ devotionals: _____

What the Lord said to me today:

_____
_____
_____
_____
_____
_____
_____
_____
_____
_____

Dear Lord,

_____
_____
_____
_____
_____
_____
_____
_____
_____
_____
_____
_____

Prayer Requests:

_____
_____
_____

Action Items:

_____
_____
_____
_____

MY TIME WITH THE LORD

date: _____

scriptures: _____ *devotionals:* _____

What the Lord said to me today:

_____
_____
_____
_____
_____
_____
_____
_____
_____
_____

Dear Lord,

_____
_____
_____
_____
_____
_____
_____
_____
_____
_____

Prayer Requests:

_____
_____
_____

Action Items:

_____
_____
_____
_____

MY TIME WITH THE LORD

date: _____

scriptures: _____ devotionals: _____

What the Lord said to me today:

_____
_____
_____
_____
_____
_____
_____
_____
_____
_____

Dear Lord,

_____
_____
_____
_____
_____
_____
_____
_____
_____
_____
_____

Prayer Requests:

_____
_____
_____

Action Items:

_____
_____
_____
_____

MY TIME WITH THE LORD

date: _____

scriptures: _____ devotionals: _____

What the Lord said to me today:

_____

_____

_____

_____

_____

_____

_____

_____

_____

_____

Dear Lord,

_____

_____

_____

_____

_____

_____

_____

_____

_____

_____

_____

Prayer Requests:

_____

_____

_____

Action Items:

_____

_____

_____

_____

MY TIME WITH THE LORD

date: _____

scriptures: _____ devotionals: _____

What the Lord said to me today:

_____
_____
_____
_____
_____
_____
_____
_____
_____
_____
_____

Dear Lord,

_____
_____
_____
_____
_____
_____
_____
_____
_____
_____
_____
_____
_____

Prayer Requests:

_____
_____
_____

Action Items:

_____
_____
_____
_____

MY TIME WITH THE LORD

date: _____

scriptures: _____ *devotionals:* _____

What the Lord said to me today:

_____
_____
_____
_____
_____
_____
_____
_____
_____
_____
_____

Dear Lord,

_____
_____
_____
_____
_____
_____
_____
_____
_____
_____
_____
_____

Prayer Requests:

_____
_____
_____

Action Items:

_____
_____
_____
_____

MY TIME WITH THE LORD

date: _____

scriptures: _____ devotionals: _____

What the Lord said to me today:

_____
_____
_____
_____
_____
_____
_____
_____
_____
_____
_____

Dear Lord,

_____
_____
_____
_____
_____
_____
_____
_____
_____
_____
_____
_____

Prayer Requests:

_____
_____
_____

Action Items:

_____
_____
_____
_____

MY TIME WITH THE LORD

date: _____

scriptures: _____ devotionals: _____

What the Lord said to me today:

_____
_____
_____
_____
_____
_____
_____
_____
_____
_____
_____

Dear Lord,

_____
_____
_____
_____
_____
_____
_____
_____
_____
_____
_____
_____
_____

Prayer Requests:

_____
_____
_____

Action Items:

_____
_____
_____
_____

MY TIME WITH THE LORD

date: _____

scriptures: _____ devotionals: _____

What the Lord said to me today:

_____
_____
_____
_____
_____
_____
_____
_____
_____
_____
_____

Dear Lord,

_____
_____
_____
_____
_____
_____
_____
_____
_____
_____
_____
_____

Prayer Requests:

_____
_____
_____

Action Items:

_____
_____
_____
_____

MY TIME WITH THE LORD

date: _____

scriptures: _____ devotionals: _____

What the Lord said to me today:

_____
_____
_____
_____
_____
_____
_____
_____
_____
_____
_____

Dear Lord,

_____
_____
_____
_____
_____
_____
_____
_____
_____
_____
_____
_____

Prayer Requests:

_____
_____
_____

Action Items:

_____
_____
_____
_____

MY TIME WITH THE LORD

date: _____

scriptures: _____ devotionals: _____

What the Lord said to me today:

_____
_____
_____
_____
_____
_____
_____
_____
_____
_____

Dear Lord,

_____
_____
_____
_____
_____
_____
_____
_____
_____
_____
_____

Prayer Requests:

_____
_____
_____

Action Items:

_____
_____
_____
_____

MY TIME WITH THE LORD

date: _____

scriptures: _____ devotionals: _____

What the Lord said to me today:

_____
_____
_____
_____
_____
_____
_____
_____
_____
_____
_____

Dear Lord,

_____
_____
_____
_____
_____
_____
_____
_____
_____
_____
_____

Prayer Requests:

_____
_____
_____

Action Items:

_____
_____
_____
_____

MY TIME WITH THE LORD

date: _____

scriptures: _____ devotionals: _____

What the Lord said to me today:

_____
_____
_____
_____
_____
_____
_____
_____
_____
_____

Dear Lord,

_____
_____
_____
_____
_____
_____
_____
_____
_____
_____
_____
_____

Prayer Requests:

_____
_____
_____

Action Items:

_____
_____
_____
_____

MY TIME WITH THE LORD

date: _____

scriptures: _____ devotionals: _____

What the Lord said to me today:

_____
_____
_____
_____
_____
_____
_____
_____
_____
_____
_____

Dear Lord,

_____
_____
_____
_____
_____
_____
_____
_____
_____
_____
_____
_____

Prayer Requests:

_____
_____
_____

Action Items:

_____
_____
_____
_____

MY TIME WITH THE LORD

date: _____

scriptures: _____ devotionals: _____

What the Lord said to me today:

_____
_____
_____
_____
_____
_____
_____
_____
_____
_____
_____

Dear Lord,

_____
_____
_____
_____
_____
_____
_____
_____
_____
_____
_____
_____
_____

Prayer Requests:

_____
_____
_____

Action Items:

_____
_____
_____
_____

MY TIME WITH THE LORD

date: _____

scriptures: _____ devotionals: _____

What the Lord said to me today:

_____
_____
_____
_____
_____
_____
_____
_____
_____
_____

Dear Lord,

_____
_____
_____
_____
_____
_____
_____
_____
_____
_____
_____

Prayer Requests:

_____
_____
_____

Action Items:

_____
_____
_____
_____

Devotional

Self-Improvement _____

Short-term goals	Long-term goals

www.ingramcontent.com/pod-product-compliance
Lightning Source LLC
Chambersburg PA
CBHW081337090426
42737CB00017B/3186